PLANET EARTH

THE WATER CYCLE

By Amy Bauma

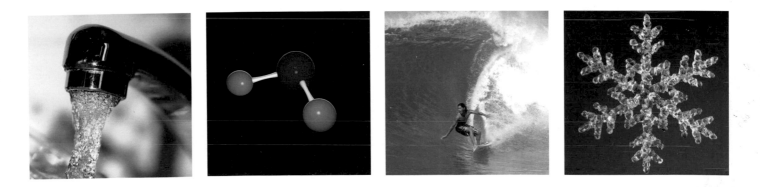

ticktock

Copyright © ticktock Entertainment Ltd 2008

First published in Great Britain in 2008 by ticktock Media Ltd,
2 Orchard Business Centre, North Farm Road, Tunbridge Wells, Kent, TN2 3XF

ticktock project editor: Ruth Owen
ticktock picture researcher: Lizzie Knowles
ticktock project designer: Emma Randall
With thanks to: Suzy Gazlay, Mark Sachner and Helen Bilton

ISBN 978 1 84696 521 0 pbk
ISBN 978 1 84696 693 4 hbk
Printed in China

A CIP catalogue record for this book is available from the British Library.

Picture credits (t=top; b=bottom; c=centre; l=left; r=right):
Alamy: 29 main. FLPA: 13bl. Corbis: 11cr, 16–17main. Getty Images: 20t, 27l. istock: 29 cr. Johnny Johnson: 10/11 main. Jiang Kehong/Xinhua Press/Corbis: 16/17 main. Daniel Kerek/ Alamy: 12 main NASA: 5tc, 9bl, 17br. NHPA: 16bl. PlanetObserver – www.planetobserver.com: 6cl. Rex Features: 28 all. Shutterstock: OFC all, 1 all, 3, 4l, 4tc, 4cc, 4bc, 4–5 main, 5tr, 5cr, 5br, 6tl, 6bl, 6–7 main, 7b, 8–9 main, 9tr, 9br, 10tl, 10cl. 10bl, 11c, 14tl, 14cl, 14–15 main, 15b, 16tl, 16cl, 18tl, 18cl, 18bl, 18–19 main, 19b, 20cl, 20bl, 21b, 22tl, 22bl, 23 main, 26clt, 26clb, 26 main, 27tr, 27cr, 29tr, 30 all, 31 all, OBC all. Science Photo Library: 12tl, 12cl, 12bl, 19tr. Superstock: 9cr, 22br. ticktock Media Ltd: 4bl, 7tr, 13t, 15t, 21 map, 23r.

Every effort has been made to trace copyright holders, and we apologise in advance for any omissions.
We would be pleased to insert the appropriate acknowledgments in any subsequent edition of this publication.

CONTENTS

Plants absorb water through their leaves and roots.

Doctors say we should drink six glasses of water each day.

Like humans, all mammals must drink regular quantities of water.

For many living things, water is home!

CHAPTER 1:
The Blue Planet

We swim in it. We bathe in it. Our landscape is carved and changed by it. Sometimes it pours from the sky, and sometimes it falls as cold, soft snowflakes. Without it, plants, animals and people could not survive. Water!

WATER, WATER EVERYWHERE

Our Earth is often called 'The Blue Planet'. This nickname comes from the fact that 71 percent of the Earth's surface is covered with water. Scientists have found some evidence showing that Mars may have had liquid water in the past. As far as we know, however, Earth is the only planet in the solar system that has water.

Water carries minerals and chemicals dissolved in it. It can dissolve more substances than any other liquid. Rivers and rainwater carries substances from the surrounding landscape into large bodies of water, such as lakes.

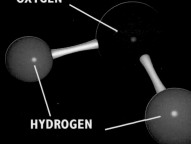

OXYGEN

HYDROGEN

H_2O—THE WATER MOLECULE

The scientific symbol for water is H_2O. The H tells us that water contains hydrogen. The O tells us that water contains oxygen. The 2 after the H tells us that each water molecule has two atoms of hydrogen for every one atom of oxygen.

The Earth is a closed system. It rarely gains or loses extra matter. This means that the same water that existed on Earth at the time of the dinosaurs is still on Earth today!

WATER AT WORK

Inside your body, water carries substances to where they are needed. It transports oxygen, and nutrients from your food. It also moisturises your skin, and carries away waste.

A KEY INGREDIENT

Your blood (as above) is 83% water.
Your brain is 75% water.
Your bones are 25% water.

WATER WAYS

You can get some of your recommended daily water intake from food. Fruits and vegetables contain lots of water, especially cucumbers and melons. In fact a watermelon is over 95% water!

Water is in the oceans, the rivers and streams. It's frozen in glaciers and at the Earth's poles. People use pumps and pipes to bring underground water up to the surface. Plants draw up water using their roots. High above our planet's surface water gathers in rainclouds. Close to the ground it floats as fog.

ESSENTIAL FOR LIFE

Water is essential to all living things on Earth. You could live without food for a month. But you could only survive for about a week without water! You are even made mostly of water. About 70 percent of an adult's body is water.

SALT WATER RECORDS

THE LARGEST OCEAN
The Pacific is Earth's largest Ocean with an area of 155,557,000 square kilometres. This ocean's total area is greater than the area of all the dry land on Earth.

CASPIAN SEA

LARGEST SALTWATER LAKE
The world's largest saltwater lake is the Caspian Sea. Its surface covers 386,400 square kilometres. This is larger than the area of the UK.

THE SALTIEST SEA
The Dead Sea, between Israel and Jordan, is the saltiest body of water in the world. Its water is nine times saltier than most seawater. This makes it very easy for people to float in the water.

EARTH'S SALT WATER
Around 97 percent of Earth's water is in the planet's oceans and seas. There are five oceans around the world. They are all linked together to form a single, large mass of salt water. The oceans are also joined to seas – smaller, shallower areas of salt water.

SALTY OCEANS AND SEAS
Seawater is mostly hydrogen and oxygen. It also contains small amounts of other elements. Two of these – sodium and chlorine – make up the salt we use to season our food. As rivers and streams rush to the sea, they carry soil and rock containing these elements and others such calcium, magnesium and potassium. Some of these materials fall to the ocean bed. Other materials, like salt, dissolve in the water. This is what makes oceans and seas salty.

Earth's oceans contain trenches deeper than Mount Everest is high. Beneath the surface are tall volcanoes and vast underwater mountain ranges. Humans have explored less than 10% of the oceans' depths.

OCEANS OF THE WORLD

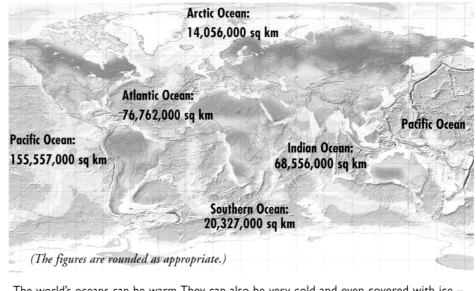

Arctic Ocean:
14,056,000 sq km

Atlantic Ocean:
76,762,000 sq km

Pacific Ocean

Pacific Ocean:
155,557,000 sq km

Indian Ocean:
68,556,000 sq km

Southern Ocean:
20,327,000 sq km

(The figures are rounded as appropriate.)

The world's oceans can be warm. They can also be very cold and even covered with ice – especially toward the poles. Around 80% of all life on Earth is found under the oceans.

THE OCEANS AT WORK

The temperatures of Earth's atmosphere and land are affected by energy from the Sun. The temperature of the oceans are affected in the same way. Shallow water in hot areas like the Persian Gulf can be as warm as 36° Celsius. However deep water is much cooler, and most ocean water is between 0 and 3° Celcius. Air and water currents circulate the Sun's heat around the globe. This helps keep ocean temperatures from being extremely cold during the winter or extremely hot during the summer.

And when energy from the Sun heats up seawater around the world, the oceans play their part in the Earth's water cycle.

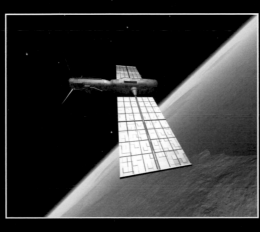

STUDYING THE OCEANS

Satellites orbit our planet hundreds of kilometres above the Earth's surface. Today, instruments on satellites can measure the surface temperature of the ocean to within 0.5° Celsius. They can provide information on surface winds, wave heights and even where fish can be found. It can take a ship weeks or months to travel across the globe, but satellites can give us information about all the world's oceans in just a few days or weeks.

WATER ON EARTH

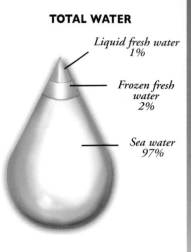

TOTAL WATER

Liquid fresh water
1%

Frozen fresh
water
2%

Sea water
97%

EARTH'S FRESH WATER

Rivers and lakes
0.3%

Other
0.9%

Groundwater
30.1%

Ice sheets
and glaciers
68.7%

EARTH'S FRESH WATER

Only three percent of the water on Earth is fresh water – water that is not salty. About one percent is liquid fresh water that plants, humans and animals can use.

LIQUID FRESH WATER

Liquid fresh water is found in lakes, rivers, streams and ponds. Fresh water is also found underground. In fact, there is 100 times more fresh water underground than in all the Earth's rivers and lakes put together. This groundwater is stored in aquifers. An aquifer is a natural underground reservoir. Water seeps into the ground and is stored between layers of gravel and rock particles. It is also stored in permeable rock. This type of rock has a structure that allows water to move through it. Think of a bath sponge, but much harder!

FROZEN FRESH WATER

About two thirds of Earth's fresh water is frozen solid in glaciers and in the polar ice caps.

Around 10 percent of the Earth's landmass is currently covered with glaciers. These vast, slow-moving rivers of frozen ice can range in size from a football field to over 160 kilometres long. Some of the water on Earth has been frozen for a very long time. Ice at the base of the ice caps in the Canadian Arctic is over 100,000 years old.

The Hubbard Glacier in Alaska stretches 22 kilometres from its starting point on Mount Logan to the sea at Yakutat Bay and Disenchantment Bay. Its front edge, or face, is over 9 kilometres wide. As it slowly moves it carves and erodes the landscape around it.

FRESH WATER RECORDS

LONGEST RIVER
The River Nile in Africa is the world's longest river. It measures 6,670 kilometres.

GREATEST RIVER BY VOLUME
The River Amazon in South America has the largest amount of water flowing in it of any river on Earth. If all the water flowing in rivers was combined, 20 percent would be in the Amazon. It pours 151,000 litres of water into the Atlantic Ocean every second.

LARGEST LAKE BY VOLUME
Lake Baikal in Russia is the world's largest freshwater lake by volume. It contains about 20 percent of the fresh water on Earth.

THE GREAT LAKES

The Great Lakes is a group of five freshwater lakes on the border between the USA and Canada. The lakes and their connecting rivers make up Earth's largest freshwater system. It contains 20 percent of the world's fresh water. If all the water in the Great Lakes was spread across the USA, the country would be nearly 3 metres deep in water!

SUPERIOR

HURON

MICHIGAN

ONTARIO

ERIE

Lake Superior is the world's largest freshwater lake. It has an area of 82,000 square kilometres.

A UNIQUE SUBSTANCE

Water is one of many different substances found naturally on Earth. Some natural substances are gases. Others are liquids or solids. Many of these substances are found in one form and can be changed into another. But water is the only substance that can be found naturally, at ordinary temperatures, in all three states of matter.

A LIQUID
Water is found in its liquid state when its temperature is between 1°C and 100°C.

A GAS
When the temperature of water rises above 100°C, water changes into a gas called water vapour.

A SOLID
When the temperature of water drops to 0°C it freezes into a solid called ice.

CHAPTER 2:
The Water Cycle

The water on Earth today is all the water that has ever been on Earth. It is important to remember that all the water we will ever be able to use is what is on the planet or in the atmosphere right now.

AN ENDLESS CYCLE

The water on our planet is constantly going through a huge recycling process called the water cycle. Think about the water you drank today. It could be the same water that your grandfather drank as a boy, or that Michelangelo used to wash his paintbrushes 500 years ago! The water cycle moves water from the oceans up into the atmosphere, down to the land and back again. But many factors can upset the balance of this cycle – especially people wasting or polluting water.

Icebergs are enormous chunks of ice that have broken off glaciers in the Arctic and Antarctic. They are made of pure, frozen fresh water. The Arctic region produces up to 50,000 icebergs a year. The Antarctic region produces too many to count!

It's important to remember that there is no more water. We cannot grow it, and we cannot manufacture it. If the water cycle is disrupted, all living things on Earth will be affected. That's why it's important to understand water and how the water cycle works.

A SPECIAL SUBSTANCE

Water is a very special substance. It is the only substance naturally found in three different states of matter. It can be a liquid – water. It can be a gas – water vapour. Or it can be a solid – ice. And it changes easily from one form to another. This ability to change form makes the water cycle possible.

Just enjoyed that swig of water from your glass? Perhaps that mouthful of water was last used by an elephant taking a bath!

ICE ON TOP

When most liquids cool, the molecules they are made from squeeze together more tightly and become more dense. But water behaves differently to all other liquids. Water molecules expand by about 9 percent as they freeze. Therefore, frozen water is much less dense than liquid water. This is why ice floats on water. It also means that water freezes on the top of a container, or a body of water such as a lake, before it freezes at the bottom. This is good news for fish and water animals. They can live under the floating ice.

WATER VAPOUR

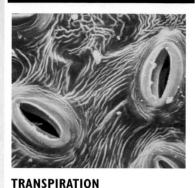

TRANSPIRATION
Plants give off water vapour through pores (tiny holes) in their leaves. These pores are known as stomates. This image shows plant pores magnified times 715 under a scanning electron microscope.

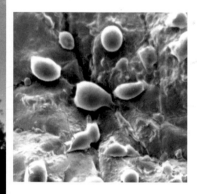

PERSPIRATION
Perspiration, or sweat, is one way that humans put water vapour into the air. The image above shows sweat beads on skin under a scanning electron microscope. The image has been magnified x 15.

BREATHING
On a cold day you can see the water vapour in your breath. We lose about 250 millilitres of water from our bodies by breathing every day.

THE WATER CYCLE – EVAPORATION
Water moves into the water cycle from sources all over the Earth. Heat from the Sun constantly warms up water on the Earth's surface and turns the liquid water into water vapour. This invisible gas then rises up into the sky and is absorbed into the atmosphere. This part of the water cycle is the evaporation stage.

WHERE DOES THE WATER COME FROM?
About 80 percent of the water vapour in the air comes from the oceans. But water also evaporates from lakes and rivers. It even evaporates from the ground. Next time you see a small puddle on the pavement near your house, notice how it soon disappears when the Sun shines. That's because it has evaporated. Water evaporates faster on a hot day, but even when it is cold evaporation takes place.

Plants, animals and people contribute to water vapour in the air, too. When people or animals breathe out they release water vapour into the atmosphere in their breath.

The Earth's atmosphere protects us from the Sun's harmful rays. At the same time, it lets enough of the Sun's heat energy through to evaporate water and drive the water cycle.

THE WATER CYCLE

THIS DIAGRAM SHOWS ALL THE STAGES OF THE WATER CYCLE. IT IS A NEVER-ENDING PROCESS.

3) RAINDROPS FALL TO GROUND

Slowly, the water droplets join together. The drops get bigger and heavier until they fall to the ground as rain. Water can also fall as other forms of precipitation, such as snow, sleet, or hail.

2) VAPOUR COOLS AND TURNS TO WATER

The warm water vapour rises. Mountains and hills direct air currents upwards, where it is cooler. Here the water vapour cools further. The vapour condenses into tiny water droplets, which we see as clouds. This is called condensation

1) THE SUN HEATS SURFACE WATER

Heat from the Sun turns water on the Earth's surface into vapour. This is called evaporation. About 80 percent of the water in the air comes from the ocean, but it also evaporates from lakes, ponds, rivers, reservoirs, puddles, and even plants and animals.

4) RAINWATER FLOWS INTO LAKES AND THE SEA

The water falls into rivers and streams. Some water sinks into the ground. Gravity causes most rainwater to flow down to the sea. When precipitation gathers on Earth's surface, it is ready to go through the cycle all over again. The process of water gathering, for example in the ocean, is called accumulation.

TRANSPIRATION

A plant absorbs water from the soil through its roots. The water is carried through the plant, along very thin tubes. The water delivers moisture and nutrients to the plant. Eventually the plant gives off water vapour from its leaves. This process is called transpiration. The air in a rainforest is almost always very humid. This is because there are so many plants in one place and they are all giving off water vapour.

CONDENSATION IN ACTION

DEW
Dew is water that condenses at ground level on warm nights. As the ground gets cold, it cools the air, too. Warm water vapour condenses on grass, rocks, and other surfaces.

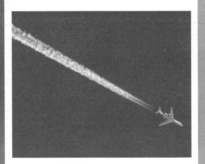

CONTRAILS
The trails that planes sometimes leave behind them are known as contrails. That's short for condensation trails. These cloud-like trails occur when water vapour in the hot exhaust from the plane meets cold air at high altitudes. The hot water vapour condenses into liquid cloud droplets.

ALL STEAMED UP!
Ever noticed how people's eyeglasses sometimes steam up? This can happen if you go from a cold place to a warm one. Warm water vapour in the air meets the cool surface of the glasses and condenses into water droplets.

THE WATER CYCLE – CONDENSATION

As the warm water vapour rises, winds move it about in the atmosphere. Mountains and hills also force air currents upward. The water vapour rises higher and higher. You would think that with all that evaporation going on our atmosphere would contain a lot of water. But only a tiny fraction – less than one percent of our atmosphere – is made up of water vapour.

As the water vapour gets higher into the atmosphere, the temperature becomes colder. The water vapour cools down and becomes drops of liquid water again. This is called condensation. It is the opposite of evaporation.

Clouds may look light and fluffy, but an average cloud can weigh as much as a Boeing-747 jumbo jet! Thankfully the warm rising air that carried the water vapour up, helps to keep the cloud in the air.

MAKING CLOUDS

The droplets of water begin to collect. They gather around dust, salt, and other tiny particles in the air. We see these gatherings of water droplets as clouds. But even when there are no clouds, the vapour is there. The droplets are just too small to be seen.

It takes millions of these cloud droplets to form just one raindrop. But eventually, the drops get bigger and heavier. The clouds become saturated. This means they have as many droplets as they can hold. Now it is time for the water to return to Earth.

HOW QUICKLY DOES WATER EVAPORATE?

Materials needed
- A wide shallow container
- A narrow, deeper container

1) Measure half a cup of water and pour this amount into both containers.

2) Place both containers in a warm, sunny place.

3) After a few hours, compare the amount of water in each container. What do you observe?

 The evaporation rate of water depends on several factors. One of these is the amount of surface area open to the air. Under similar conditions, water from a wide, shallow lake will evaporate more quickly than water in a narrower, deeper lake.

INVESTIGATING CONDENSATION

Materials needed
- Two glasses, jars or other see-through glass containers
- Room temperature water
- Ice water

1) Fill one glass with room temperature water. Fill the other glass with ice water.

2) What do you observe happening? Where are the droplets coming from?

Warm water vapour condenses when it comes into contact with something cold.

Snowflakes always have six sides. No two snowflakes are alike.

Raindrops really ARE shaped like drops. The effect of gravity on the raindrops is to 'drag' them into a drop form. Without gravity acting on them, raindrops would be more rounded.

THE WATER CYCLE – PRECIPITATION

The cooler the air gets, the less moisture it is able to hold. Sooner or later, the gathering water becomes heavy enough to fall back to Earth. This is called precipitation. Rain is the most common form of precipitation. But the moisture can also take the form of snow, hail and sleet. All of these are types of precipitation.

RAIN AND SNOW

Raindrops form when colliding cloud droplets combine. It takes about a million cloud droplets to make just one raindrop. Snowflakes form when the air temperature falls below freezing at 0°C. The cloud droplets turn into ice crystals. As more water then freezes on the ice crystals, they grow bigger. As the crystals fall down through the clouds, they knock into other crystals and form snowflakes.

The speed at which rain falls depends on the size of the raindrops. Heavy rain can fall at speeds up to 90 kilometres per hour!

KEEPING THE BALANCE

Different areas around the world get different amounts of rain. But sometimes an area will receive either no rain, or less rain than usual. Too little rain can cause a drought. People and animals cannot find water to drink and crops cannot grow. This can lead to a famine. Too much rain can cause flooding. Rivers can burst their banks and sometimes 'flash floods' occur when the ground cannot soak up the rain quickly enough. Floods can wipe out crops, damage homes, and cost lives. Water is essential to life, but the amount of it must be balanced.

BACK DOWN TO EARTH

Over time, the amount of water that falls as precipitation across the globe is exactly the same as the amount that evaporates. For the water that falls in the ocean, the water cycle is complete and will begin again. Water that falls on the land, however, still has some way to go to complete its cycle.

RAINFALL RECORDS

GREATEST 24 HOUR DOWNPOUR

The record for the greatest amount of rainfall during a single 24-hour period goes to Foc-Foc in Réunion, Africa. Between 7 January and 8 January 1966, 182.5 centimetres of rain was recorded.

MOST RAIN IN A YEAR

The most rain to fall in one place in a year was recorded at Cherrapunji in North Eastern India. During 1861, 2,300 centimetres of rain fell.

WORLD'S RAINIEST PLACE

One of the world's rainiest places is Mount Wai'ale'ale in Hawaii. The average annual rainfall is about 1,140 centimetres. As warm air passes over the island it meets the steep sides of the mountain and rises quickly. This causes lots of fast condensation to happen. This means lots of precipitation in one spot.

MOUNT WAI'ALE'ALE

KAUAI

ACCUMULATION

STREAMS AND RIVERS

Small trickles of water move downhill and join bigger flows. Channels and valleys in the Earth's surface become gathering places for moving water. These gathering places become rivers constantly moving downhill towards the oceans.

GROUNDWATER AND UNDERGROUND STREAMS

Water in aquifers slowly trickles downhill between the cracks in underground rocks. This water may become an underground stream. However, eventually it will join a body of water on the surface.

LAKES AND PONDS

Gravity keeps water constantly moving downwards. But the uneven surface of the Earth traps water in dips where it forms lakes or ponds.

THE WATER CYCLE – ACCUMULATION

Every raindrop or snowflake that falls to Earth is on its way to join the final stage of the water cycle. This stage, the gathering of water back on Earth, is called the accumulation stage. Some water that falls on the land will run off into streams, rivers and lakes. Some water will be absorbed and become groundwater in aquifers.

WATER ON THE MOVE

Gravity keeps water moving downward towards the oceans. Melting snow and ice flows down mountains and forms streams. Rivers and streams flow across the land to join the sea. Groundwater moves slowly underground to join rivers or flow into the ocean.

GLACIER

MOUNTAIN RANGE
Melting snow joins streams and rivers, or seeps into the ground.

VALLEY

GROUNDWATER
Rain seeps into the soil and becomes groundwater.

No matter where it falls, all of the water will eventually make its way back to the oceans to complete one circuit of the water cycle.

REJOINING THE WATER CYCLE

Rain that falls on a warm day could potentially rejoin the water cycle almost immediately, by evaporating again. But not all water that falls on Earth rejoins the cycle at this pace. Some water might seep deep underground and stay there for thousands of years. Some snowflakes might freeze and stay trapped in a glacier for hundreds of years. A drop of water at the bottom of the ocean may be there for centuries before it reaches the water's surface, evaporates and rejoins the cycle. In fact, a water molecule can spend millions of years at the accumulation stage.

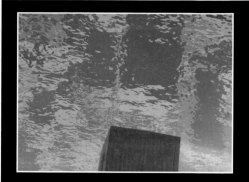

MELTDOWN!

Global warming is the gradual warming up of our Earth. One effect of our Earth getting warmer will be the melting of ice stored in the Earth's glaciers. If all this ice stored in glaciers melted, the Earth's oceans would rise by about 70 metres! Many towns and cities around the world are built at sea level or just above sea level. This means the land they are built on is at the same level as the ocean's surface. Even a rise in the ocean's surface of just three metres would mean that cities such as London and New York would be under water.

STREAM
A mountain stream will eventually join a river.

RIVER
A river winds across the land until it joins the ocean.

OCEAN

Just 0.01 square kilometres of Amazon rainforest in South America can contain up to 1500 different plant species.

At night, the desert gets cold. Water vapour in the air condenses into water on the spikes of plants like the saguaro cactus. The water then trickles onto the ground to be collected by the plant's roots.

Camels live in hot deserts. They close their nostrils between breaths. This stops water evaporating from their noses.

DISTRIBUTION OF EARTH'S WATER

Water is not distributed equally over the Earth's landmasses. Some parts of the world receive rain almost every day. Others may go weeks, months or even years without rain. Water is an essential factor in all Earth's ecosystems. The number and types of plants and animals a place can support are affected by access to water.

WATER TO SPARE

As the Sun shines down on the plants and trees of a rainforest, huge amounts of water vapour rise into the atmosphere. In turn, this creates huge quantities of rain. The Earth's rainforests support millions of different plant and animal species because water is plentiful.

LIMITED WATER SUPPLIES

Deserts are places where there is less than 25 centimetres of rainfall each year. Fewer animals and plants can survive here. Those that do have adapted to deal with the limited water supply. Some desert plants, such as the saguaro cactus, have spiky leaves with very little surface area. This stops too much water evaporating from the plant.

WATER AND BIOMES

We separate the world into large regions called biomes. Each type of biome has the same kind of weather and climate. Plants, animals and people adapt their lives according to the availability of water in the biome where they live.

BIOMES – WATER AND SURVIVAL

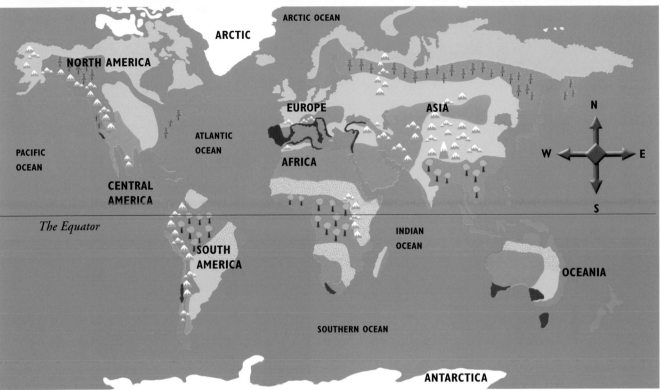

ARCTIC OCEAN

ARCTIC

NORTH AMERICA

EUROPE

ASIA

ATLANTIC
OCEAN

PACIFIC
OCEAN

AFRICA

CENTRAL
AMERICA

The Equator

SOUTH
AMERICA

INDIAN
OCEAN

OCEANIA

N
W E
S

SOUTHERN OCEAN

ANTARCTICA

 TEMPERATE GRASSLANDS
Warm, dry summers, cool or cold winters; rainfall supports lots of plant and animal life

SAVANNA
Large plains with scattered trees and bushes; amount of foliage determined by extent of rainfall

 DESERT
Dry land, little rain; plants, include cacti that store water

TUNDRA
Cold, windy plains; soil freezes just below surface; plants need short roots to absorb nutrients

ARCTIC/ANTARCTICA
Cold and dry all year; frozen ground and icy seas; animals live off rich marine life

OCEAN
Saltwater environment supports enormous variety of marine life

CHAPARRAL
Shrubby coastal area; plants and animals adapted to hot, dry summers, mild winters

 TEMPERATE DECIDUOUS FOREST
Plants bloom and thrive in summer, and are usually dormant in winter

CONIFEROUS FOREST
Cold evergreen forest; most animals migrate or hibernate in winter

TROPICAL RAINFOREST
Hot, wet climate, with lots of sun and rain supporting huge variety of life

Precipitation is low in the Arctic. Most precipitation falls as snow. Arctic animals, such as polar bears, are surrounded by snow and ice, so they rarely drink. They have adapted to get the water they need from their food.

Water, with the help of the wind, shapes cliffs and shores along a Hawaiian coast. The Na Pali coast of the island of Kauai is known for its breathtaking cliffs.

CHAPTER 3:
Water in Action

The water cycle is all about water changing between states of matter. During the cycle, water changes from a liquid to a gas and back again. Sometimes it also becomes a solid. As the Earth's water goes through this process plants, animals and people use the water in its three states. The water is also busy changing the face of the Earth.

SHAPING OUR WORLD

The oceans pull and push at the edges of the land, reshaping whole coastlines and cutting craggy cliffs into them.

The ground and rocky landforms, such as mountains, are weathered and eroded by rain or river water. This means they are worn away until they become crumbly. Then rainwater, or riverwater carries the sediment away to a new place.

Rivers carve V-shaped valleys into the crust of the Earth over many, many years. Frozen water in the form of glaciers slowly moves over the Earth's surface leaving behind U-shaped valleys.

The Grand Canyon in Arizona, USA, was carved from the surrounding rock by the flow of the Colorado River. In its deepest places the gorge is 1,800 metres deep.

A U-shaped glacial valley in Switzerland.

Water movement below Earth's surface causes erosion, too. It works the same as it does at the surface. Here it has carved out a large underground cave. Water running underground can create incredible features such as stalactites (seen here) and stalagmites. These are formed by dripping water which contains calcium salts.

HOW DOES WATER SHAPE THE LAND?

Materials needed
- A rectangular tray with sides
- Water
- Two long, narrow wooden blocks
- Sand

1) Fill the tray with the sand.

2) Set one end of the tray on the wooden blocks so that the tray is sitting at a slant.

3) Slowly pour a stream of water into the tray at the high end. What do you observe happening?

Even a small, slow trickle of water has the power to make changes to the Earth's surface. These changes can happen fast, for example during a flood. Or they can happen gradually over millions of years.

4) Experiment with shaping the 'terrain'. Add some obstructions to your stream of water and observe what happens.

5) You can try the same experiment using a bar of soap to simulate the path of a glacier. Place the soap at the top of the tray and move it slowly downwards over the sand. What do you observe? How is the path carved by the bar of soap different to the path carved by the water?

WATER AT WORK

LIVESTOCK FARMING
Water is needed to raise livestock, such as sheep, cows and chickens. A dairy cow needs to drink 18 litres of water to produce 4.5 litres of milk.

INDUSTRIAL USES
Probably every product that is manufactured in a factory has water used in the manufacturing process at some point. Water is used for processing, washing and cooling. It is even used for transporting the finished products by ship. About 1 billion litres of water are used every day to produce all the newspapers printed in the USA.

HUMAN USES OF WATER
People have always needed water to drink and for basic survival. Water has been used for thousands of years for washing, growing crops, and raising animals. In addition to these basic needs, people use water for transportation and shipping goods. Look on a world map and see how many major cities are built on rivers and lakes or close to the ocean. Today, around 90 percent of all goods traded between countries are still transported by ships.

ADVANCES WITH WATER
Today, human ingenuity combined with technology have found new ways to make water work for us. Huge dams change the courses of rivers and collect the water in reservoirs. The water is passed through a water purification system to remove disease-causing organisms, chemicals and pollutants. Then the clean water is pumped directly to our homes.

Hydroelectric power plants are built over flowing rivers. First the water is stored behind a dam. Then as the water is released, the movement turns huge turbine blades. This, in turn generates electricity.

In temperate biomes there is enough natural rainfall to grow crops. Today we can grow crops even in hot, dry places with little rainfall. Water is pumped from rivers, lakes, reservoirs and wells to irrigate crops. About 60 percent of the world's use of fresh water is for irrigating crops.

And we use water for fun! Cruise ships and jetskis dot our oceans, while swimming pools and hot tubs are a great way to relax.

WASTEWATER

Waste from animals (such as urine and droppings) passes back into the ground naturally. Human waste, and dirty water from industry should be cleaned before it is returned back into the water cycle. Wastewater usually travels to sewage treatment plants through underground pipes. At the treatment plant large pieces of waste are removed. The water then passes through a system of tanks containing tiny organisms that feed on the sewage. The organisms break down the sewage and make it harmless. Then the water is clean enough to return to a river or to the sea.

One method of irrigating crops in dry areas is the centre-pivot irrigation system. It uses moving spray guns that pivot around a central water source. From the air the irrigated circles show up as green.

WATER IN THE HOME

Here are some common uses of water in the home. Also shown is the average amount of water each activity uses.

- One bath: 80 litres

- One shower: 35 litres

- One toilet flush: 8 litres

- One dishwasher load: 25 litres

- One washing machine load: 65 litres

Calculate how much water you use in a single day.

AVERAGE USES OF WATER IN THE HOME

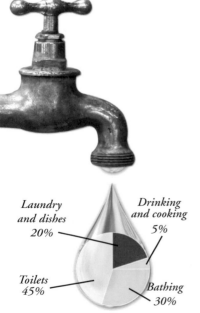

Laundry and dishes 20%

Drinking and cooking 5%

Toilets 45%

Bathing 30%

CHAPTER 4:
Saving Water

Water is an important natural resource. It is essential to the survival of all life on Earth. However, it is so much a part of our everyday lives that it is easy to take it for granted.

WASTING WATER

Do you have any taps that drip in your home? One drip per second means that 4 litres of water a day are escaping from your tap.

Do you leave the tap running when you brush your teeth? Running a tap for just one minute can use around 10 litres of water.

Using a hosepipe to wash the car makes the job easier, and more fun! But rinsing with a hose can use the same amount of water as over 30 buckets. Wash the car using buckets of water instead. You will use a lot less.

Many children in the third world have to walk three to four hours daily to fetch water.

An average adult in the US or UK uses between 500 and 600 litres of water a day. It pours from our taps – clean, safe and ready to use.

Many people in less developed countries around the world use only about 90 litres of water a day. That water might be in a well far from their home. And, what's more, the water could be dirty or diseased.

Around 1.2 billion people in the world today do not have access to clean water.

UNDERSTANDING EARTH'S WATER SUPPLY

Materials needed
- 18-litre bucket of water
- Tablespoon & teaspoon
- Dropper
- 3 see-through containers (such as drinking glasses). Label the containers A, B and C

1) The full bucket of water represents all the water present on Earth. Measure out 25.5 tablespoons of water into glass A. This is the water frozen in icecaps and glaciers.

2) Measure out 8 tablespoons of water from the bucket and put it into glass B. This represents groundwater.

3) Measure out half a teaspoon and add it to glass B. This represents the water held in freshwater lakes, ponds, reservoirs.

4) Measure out a drop of water and add it to glass B. This represents water in rivers, streams.

5) Measure out two drops. This represents water in the atmosphere, such as clouds, fog and rain. Add it to glass B.

6) Measure out half a teaspoon and put it in glass C. This represents water held in salt lakes and inland seas.

Look at the bucket and the three glasses. How much of this water is available for humans and animals to use as drinking water?

Only the water in glass B is available for all living things on Earth to use. And if this water is dirty it must be cleaned up (if possible) before it can be used.

WATER FOR ALL

Everyone on Earth should be able to use clean water every day.

Many organisations around the world are helping communities that do not have clean water. They raise funds to pay for wells to be dug and for water pumps and sanitation equipment to be installed.

You can help to raise money for this work. You will find information about organisations involved in this work on these websites:

www.wateraid.org

www.justadrop.org

www.charitywater.org

www.unicef.org/wes

WATER IN DANGER

Chemicals that are used in factories sometimes escape into rivers. Fertilisers used on farms can wash into freshwater supplies. These pollutants can kill plants and animals. They can ruin precious sources of valuable fresh water.

The more uses we create for water, the more demands we put on the water cycle. Every day millions of litres of fresh water are wasted in our homes and in industry. Sometimes sources of fresh water become polluted or dry up due to overuse for irrigation.

Toxic chemicals in rivers and lakes can kill huge numbers of fish. As big fish eat smaller fish, the toxic chemicals in their bodies become more concentrated, and therefore more deadly.

DESALINATION

Desalination is a process for removing salt from ocean water. It is one way to make fresh water available where it is scarce. Desalination of ocean water is common in places like the Middle East. Sixty percent of the world's desalination plants are at work there. Use of the process is growing fast in other areas of the world, as the demand for water increases. However, it is expensive to produce water in this way. In places where there is fresh water, it's better to conserve existing fresh water than look for ways to make new!

WHAT CAN WE DO?

Governments can prosecute companies who pollute water and make them pay fines.

We can ALL save water in our everyday lives.

Remember: only one percent of the water on Earth is usable fresh water. If we use the Earth's fresh water faster than nature can recycle it, there will not be enough fresh water to go around in the future.

Fresh water is vital to human, animal and plant life. It is the most valuable resource on Earth, and we must not waste it.

WATER-SAVING TIPS

TURN OFF THAT TAP!
When you are brushing your teeth, don't leave the tap running.

SAVE AS YOU FLUSH
Most households use more water flushing the toilet than anything else. Your family can install a water saving device in the toilet cistern.

BE FULLY LOADED
Make sure you organise your laundry so you don't need to wash items individually. Only use the washing machine or dishwasher when there's a full load.

WATER SAVING GARDENS
In half an hour a lawn sprinkler can use as much water as a family of four uses in a day. Many people are laying stone or wood surfaces in their gardens today. They don't need lots of water to look good. And they don't need mowing!

NO ICE PLEASE
A theme park in the USA has stopped serving ice in their drinks and is saving a massive 114,000 litres of water a year. Imagine how much water we would save if we all did without ice!

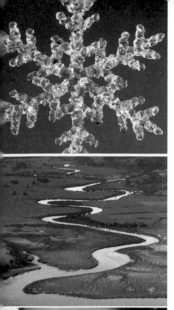

GLOSSARY

accumulation The process of something building up or collecting. In the water cycle, accumulation is the stage where water remains for a period of time underground, in the ocean, or in another body of water.

aquifer A natural underground reservoir. Water which has seeped into the ground is stored between layers of gravel or permeable rock.

atmosphere The thick layer of air that surrounds the Earth. The gases that make up Earth's atmosphere include nitrogen (78%) and oxygen (21%). There is also water, and small quantities of other gases such as argon, greenhouse gases and carbon dioxide.

atom All materials and subtances are made up of atoms. They are the smallest possible unit of an element that still behaves like that element.

biome A large geographical area with similar climate, weather, and plant and animal life. Examples of biomes include rainforest, ocean and desert.

condensation The process by which a gas changes to a liquid, such as when water vapour turns into droplets of water.

dam A barrier constructed to hold back water.

desalination The process of removing salt from sea water.

dissolving The process in which a solid combines with a liquid and forms a solution, such as salt water.

drought An unusually long period without rainfall. Droughts often cause severe water shortages and famine.

ecosystem A natural system made up of a community of plants and animals and the environment in which they live. Within an ecosystem the animals and plants rely on each other to survive. The plants and animals also rely on non-living things, such as water, the Sun and soil.

elements Substances made up of a single type of atom. Elements can't be broken into simpler components by chemical processes. There are 92 naturally occurring elements.

equator An imaginary line round Earth which is the same distance from the North and South Poles.

erosion The wearing away of material by the action of water, wind, or glacial ice.

evaporation The process by which a liquid changes to a gas, such as when liquid water turns to water vapour.

famine A severe shortage of food that can lead to starvation and disease.

flood The rising and overflowing of water onto normally dry land.

fresh water Water that is not salty, and which can be used by humans, animals, and plants. The water in ponds, lakes, rivers and streams is usually fresh water.

glacier A large body of ice that moves slowly down a slope or valley or spreads outward on the surface of the land. Some glaciers move only a few centimetres a year. Others travel up to one metre a day.

global warming A gradual warming of the Earth's atmosphere. Most scientists believe that this is partly caused by humans burning fossils fuels, such as oil and coal.

gravity Gravity is the force that pulls one mass toward another. An object with a large mass has more gravity than an object with a smaller mass. This is why objects are pulled towards Earth.

groundwater Water that has seeped through the Earth's surface and is held underground in the soil or among rocks.

hail Water droplets high in the atmosphere that have frozen. Instead of falling as raindrops, they fall as small balls of ice.

humid When the air has a lot of water vapour in it.

hydroelectric power Electricity which is generated by the movement of flowing water.

iceberg A large floating mass of ice that has broken away from an glacier. Icebergs are made of frozen fresh water. About 80 to 90% of an iceberg is under the water.

irrigation The process of bringing water to a place. For example pumping water from a river to irrigate (water) crops.

molecule A tiny particle which consists of two or more atoms bonded together. It is the smallest part of a substance that has all the characteristics of that substance.

natural resources The materials, energy sources and living things found in nature that are useful to people and other living creatures. Water, air, minerals, the Sun's energy, plants and animals are all natural resources.

perspiration Sweating – a process where water is released through pores in the skin, to help humans or animals cool down.

polar ice caps Huge permanently frozen areas of ice at the North and South Poles.

pollute To contaminate or make impure or unclean. For example, fertilisers used on farms can contaminate water, making it poisonous and killing plants and animals.

pore A tiny opening on the skin of an animal, or the leaf or stem of a plant. This opening allows water, gases, and other materials to pass in and out of the organism.

precipitation Any form of water (for example, rain or snow) that falls to Earth's surface.

purification A process where unwanted materials like pollutants and dangerous chemicals are removed from a substance.

reservoir A large natural or artificially made lake that is used to store water for supply to homes and businesses.

salt water Water, such as ocean water, that contains dissolved salts.

sleet A cold, slushy substance halfway between rain and snow. Sleet is caused by snowflakes melting as they fall to Earth because the ground temperature is above freezing.

transpiration The process by which plants give off water vapour through tiny pores in their leaves called stomates.

vapour A gas formed from a liquid that has evaporated.

wastewater Water that has been used in people's homes or in factories, which contains waste products and pollutants. It must be treated before it is returned to the water cycle.

weathering The gradual breaking down of rock. Over time, wind, water and other surface factors wear away the rock's surface until it crumbles.